Martin Taylor's

LATIN JAZZ GUITAR SOLOING ETUDES

Master The Art of Latin Jazz Guitar Soloing In 7 Beautiful Etudes

MARTIN TAYLOR

With Joseph Alexander

FUNDAMENTAL**CHANGES**

Martin Taylor's Latin Jazz Guitar Soloing Etudes

Master the Art of Latin Jazz Guitar In 7 Beautiful Etudes

ISBN: 978-1-78933-440-1

Published by www.fundamental-changes.com

Copyright © 2024 Martin Taylor and Joseph Alexander

Edited by Tim Pettingale

www.fundamental-changes.com

For over 350 free guitar lessons with videos check out:

www.fundamental-changes.com

Join our free Facebook Community of Cool Musicians

www.facebook.com/groups/fundamentalguitar

Tag us for a share on Instagram: **FundamentalChanges**

Cover Image Copyright: Author photo used by permission.

Contents

About the Authors

Dr Martin Taylor MBE is a virtuoso guitarist, composer, educator and musical innovator.

Acoustic Guitar magazine has called him THE acoustic guitarist of his generation. Chet Atkins said that Martin is one of the greatest and most impressive guitarists in the world, and Pat Metheny commented that, "Martin Taylor is one of the most awesome solo guitar players in the history of the instrument."

Widely considered to be the world's foremost exponent of solo jazz and fingerstyle guitar playing, Martin possesses an inimitable style that has earned him global acclaim from fellow musicians, fans and critics alike. He dazzles audiences with his signature style which artfully combines virtuosity, emotion and humour with a strong, engaging stage presence.

Martin has enjoyed a remarkable musical career spanning five decades, with more than 100 recordings to his credit. Completely self-taught, beginning at the early age of 4, he has pioneered a unique way of approaching solo jazz guitar that he now breaks down into seven distinct stages in order to teach others.

Martin has penned many tuition books for the guitar including:

Beyond Chord Melody

Walking Bass for Jazz Guitar

Martin Taylor Single Note Soloing for Jazz Guitar

Martin Taylor's Christmas Songs for Jazz Guitar

Martin Taylor's Complete Jazz Guitar Method Compilation

Martin Taylor's Jazz Guitar Licks Phrase Book

Martin Taylor's Advanced Jazz Guitar Licks Phrase Book

Martin Taylor's Latin Jazz Rhythm Guitar

Joseph Alexander is one of the most prolific writers of modern guitar tuition methods.

He has sold nearly 2,000,000 books that have educated and inspired a generation of upcoming musicians. His uncomplicated tuition style is based around breaking down the barriers between theory and performance, and making music accessible to all.

Educated at London's Guitar Institute and Leeds College of Music, where he earned a degree in Jazz Studies, Joseph has taught thousands of students and written over 40 books on playing the guitar.

He is the managing director of *Fundamental Changes Ltd.*, a publishing company whose sole purpose is to create the highest quality music tuition books and pay excellent royalties to writers and musicians.

Fundamental Changes has published over 300 music tuition books and is currently accepting submissions from prospective authors and teachers of all instruments.

Get in touch via **webcontact@fundamental-changes.com** if you'd like to work with us on a project.

Foreword

During my early days as a working musician, I often played at the dance functions that took place in hotel ballrooms across central London. Regularly on the setlist were tunes like *The Girl from Ipanema* and *Meditation* and I noticed that these tunes would always receive a warm response from the audience. Something about the sunny yet relaxed feel of the bossa nova really connected with people. Although I didn't do these kinds of gigs for long, as a jazz musician I grew to love the bossa – not just for its infectious rhythm, but because all the bossa standards have beautiful melodies and chord changes, which makes them fun to improvise over.

Years later, I worked with the guitarist Charlie Byrd in the group The Great Guitars. Charlie was a kind of musicologist who knew all about the music of South America, and had especially fallen in love with the music of Brazil. He, along with other important musicians of his era, was instrumental in bringing this sound to North America. His famous recordings with Stan Getz helped to popularize the form with a wider audience. To this day, if I want to create a summery, laid-back mood in our home when friends come over for dinner, I'll put on some Stan Getz and Charlie Byrd, or maybe Laurindo Almeida, for the mood their music instantly conjures up.

It's important to understand that the bossa nova can be played in dozens of subtly different ways. In fact, there are as many variations of it as there are dialects across South America, and this essentially comes down to the culture/temperament of the people in its different regions. Even within the same nation, the bossa nova of say, Sao Paolo in Brazil, is different from that of Rio de Janeiro.

In jazz, we play a homogenised bossa. It's not the most authentic representation of this music, but it's an adapted way of playing it that just fits when jazz musicians come together. When you're on a gig and someone calls a bossa, the way of playing it you'll learn here will always work.

So, this book is *not* the definitive guide to bossa nova, and I don't want you to think this is the correct or only way of playing it. Instead, think of it as a way of accessing this music and learning it in a jazz setting. For any purists who are interested in getting into Latin music in more detail, I encourage you to listen to and study the music of guitar players who grew up and developed their craft in South America. For example, check out the incredible playing of Yamandú Costa, the Brazilian 7-string virtuoso. He's one of my favourite players of this type of music!

As you work through the solo etudes presented here, remember that the main thing about the bossa nova is the *feel*. Learn the lines and solos, but above all, strive to capture the summery, laid-back vibe. Once you have that in place, you can explore all the different ways there are to embellish the lines and elevate them into something more sophisticated and personal.

Enjoy this little Latin Jazz journey!

Martin

Introduction From Joseph

In this collection, you're not just learning to play a set of tunes, you're getting a masterclass in the subtleties of Bossa Nova and Latin guitar from one of the genre's most articulate voices. For each piece in this book Martin has not only shared his personal reflections but also broken down the essence of what makes these tunes resonate so deeply.

Take *The Girl from Ipanema*, for instance. Martin dives into the sexy, jazz-infused world of major sevenths and ninths, offering insights into how these intervals colour the music and set the mood. It's like understanding why a martini can feel so right at the end of a long day. Through Martin's lens, you're not just playing chords, you're crafting an atmosphere.

Or consider *How Insensitive* and *The Shadow of Your Smile*, where Martin explores the balance between simplicity and depth, demonstrating how a tune can be straightforward yet emotionally profound. These pieces serve as perfect examples of how to navigate the nuanced landscape of Latin rhythms, keeping the sun shining through the melancholy.

And it's not just about the notes. Martin emphasizes the importance of phrasing, timing, and feeling the music. He teaches us to listen, to experiment, and to find our own voice within the framework of these classic tunes. It's a reminder that playing music is a conversation not a monologue, and that each of us has something unique to say.

From the samba-infused streets of *Triste,* to the intimate reflections of Martin's arrangement of the First World War marching tune *Keep The Home Fires Burning*, this collection is a journey through the heart of Bossa Nova and Latin music. Martin encourages us to play with the tempo, to feel the rhythm in our bodies before a note is even played, and to always keep our ears open to the endless possibilities that music offers.

As you work through these pieces, you'll not only develop your technical skills but also deepen your musical expression. Martin's guidance is like having a conversation with an old friend who happens to be a master of his craft. He doesn't just teach you how to play, he teaches you how to listen, how to feel, and ultimately, how to communicate more effectively through your instrument.

So, whether you're a seasoned player or just starting out, this book is an invitation to explore, to discover, and to fall in love with the rich, vibrant world of Bossa Nova and Latin guitar. Let Martin Taylor be your guide on this musical journey and try to capture some of his magic.

Introduction from Martin Taylor

I've spent a good chunk of my life playing guitar, diving deep into the worlds of Jazz and Bossa Nova. Let me share a bit of what I've learned along the way, especially when it comes to the Latin guitar stuff that this book is all about.

Latin music, for me, is special because it's got this groove that makes me want to play with more melody. It's different from playing straight jazz or swing where you might just barrel through. The Latin groove gives you room to breathe, to think a bit more about what you're playing, and *why*. It's like having a conversation where there's space for both sides to speak without stepping on each other's toes.

I like to think of music in terms of making a sandwich. You start with the basics – bread, butter, cheese maybe. That's your foundation. But then you experiment. You maybe throw some olives in the bread or swap the cheddar for camembert. Suddenly, you've got something different, something special. It's the same with music. You start with the basics, then mix things up until you find that perfect combo that just clicks. And it's all about trying things out, seeing what works, what doesn't, and having a bit of fun along the way.

At its core, music (especially the kind that gets your foot tapping like Bossa Nova and Latin tunes) is about movement. It's physical; it comes from a place of dance and expression. When I play, I'm not just hitting notes, I'm trying to capture that feeling of motion… of *emotion*.

So, what you're holding in your hands is more than just a collection of guitar solos – it's an invitation to explore, to play around with rhythm and melody, and to find your own way of expressing those timeless tales that music tells us. Let's dive in together and see where these tunes take us. I hope you find as much joy in playing them as I have.

What to Look Out For

This book is deliberately light on theory. We want you to learn the sound and feel of these solos rather than analyse them to death. However, there are some recuring ideas that Martin uses in his Latin playing that will help you to understand his approach. Look out for when they pop up as you go along.

Minor 9 Magic – Two Ways with The Minor 9

The m9 chord is prolific in Latin Jazz and with good reason. It lends any minor chord the cool, sophisticated edge that this music cries out for. There are two ways Martin commonly uses this sound in his solos and both are substitution ideas.

First, the idea of repurposing something we already know to easily create the minor 9 sound: playing a familiar major 7 arpeggio shape over a minor chord.

Look at bars 45 and 53 of *The Girl from Ipanema*. Study the shape of these lines and you'll see that they are Bbmaj7 arpeggios, first played ascending in bar 45, then descending in bar 53.

We all know that major 7 shape and this is a common substitution idea that works particularly well in Latin Jazz.

It works on the principle of common tones.

Bbma7 contains the notes Bb D F A

Gm7 contains the notes G Bb D F

It's the A note of the Bbmaj7 arpeggio that does all the hard work in these lines, as it's the 9th of a G minor chord. Superimposing Bbmaj7 over a G minor harmony is like playing a rootless Gm9 arpeggio. It's a beautiful sound!

Second, another popular substitution idea is playing a minor 9 arpeggio over a dominant 7 chord.

Look at bar 27 of the Ipanema solo. The chord is Eb7 and the line played is a Bbm9 arpeggio (Bb Db F Ab C). It's normal to omit the b7 (Ab) in this type of lick.

The effect of playing Bbm9 over Eb7 is to create a richer Eb13 sound.

It's another idea that works on the common tones principle, but there's an easier way to think of it. Imagine that Eb7 is a V chord, and we're just playing notes from the ii chord that would normally precede it (Bm – Eb7).

Octaves & Thirds

Martin isn't especially known for playing Wes Montgomery style octaves, but they sound especially cool and appropriate in Latin music.

Check out bars 33-34 of *How Insensitive* to hear how effectively octaves can be used in this context to conjure up the melancholy yet hopeful feeling of the tune. They are used again in bars 66-67.

How Insensitive has a complex harmony that is melody-led. In other words, the chords were written to support the meandering melody, rather than the melody being written over a set of preconceived chords.

At times, it therefore felt right to Martin to play passages in 3rds to spell out the harmony a little more – something he doesn't often do when soloing, but which suits the Latin Jazz genre. Check out the beautiful cascading line in bars 57-58 that provides an alternative way of spelling out the Cm7 to F7 harmony. And earlier, in bars 40-41, this approach breaks the Bbmaj7 chord down into smaller segments to provide a nice contrast to the arpeggiated lines that surround it.

Space and Line Length

You could say that the rhythm of Latin Jazz sways like the palm trees on Copacabana beach! This music has a natural ebb and flow, and it demands that we think differently about our phrasing.

Often, when playing Latin Jazz, Martin will construct phrases that miss out beat 1 of the bar, but then flow seamlessly over the bars that follow.

In *Night and Day*, for example, bars 5-8 provide the perfect illustration. The line over the Bmaj7 chord starts after an 1/8th note rest, on the "&" of beat 1. From there, the line flows through the next three bars with phrasing that crosses the bar line.

In bar six, a 1/4 note triplet phrase has the effect of slowing down the phrase, pulling back against the lilting pulse of the music. Then, a 1/4 note played on the "&" of beat 4 causes that note to float over the bar line into bar seven.

There are lots of other examples of this phrasing idea throughout the tune. Check out the gorgeous line that navigates the descending minor chord sequence in bars 25-29, which again starts after an 1/8th note rest and includes several notes that are held over the bar line to float over the groove.

Repeating Motifs

In a bittersweet medium-slow tune like Johnny Mandel's *The Shadow of Your Smile*, Martin's solo tells a plaintive story.

More so than the other solos you'll learn here, Martin uses repeating motif ideas for this tune – each of which take on a different meaning as the chords change beneath them. This is a classic "storytelling" device that Martin uses here to great effect.

Listen, for instance, to how he spells out the minor ii–V–i chord changes (F#m7b5 – B7 – Em7) with just two or three notes in bars 9-11.

In bars 13-15 he uses a more complex phrase with hammer-ons and pull-offs to tie together the C#m7b5 and F#7b9 chords, then moves the motif down a string to play over the F#m7b5.

Notice too, the lovely motif-based idea using two repeated notes that spans bars 45-48. This idea has a vocal quality to the phrasing and the simplicity of those notes is profound over the rich, shifting chord progression underneath.

Visualising Chord Tones

We know that jazz standards tend to have lush harmonies, but Latin standards – especially those written by Jobim – have especially rich harmonic structures for us to navigate when soloing. Plus, to make things more challenging, some of the most harmonically complex tunes are also played quite quickly! Two such tunes are *Triste* and *Wave*, both Jobim compositions.

Jobim's tunes often feature some surprise chords, which is why it's very important to have a sound understanding of the harmony before attempting a solo. In situations like these, it's important to be able to visualise the chord shapes on the neck and be able to home in on the important notes that make the sound of the chord. By "seeing" the chords and picking out the important notes, we instantly have a way of playing through the changes, spelling out the harmony.

Take the opening of the solo to *Triste*. It begins in safe territory with a Dmaj7 chord, which is immediately followed by a classic Jobim harmonic twist via a Bbmaj7#11 chord.

In bars 1-4 Martin follows a common shape for each chord and carefully selects the notes he wants to use located around each voicing.

Thinking ahead to the Bbmaj7#11, he plays an E note on the second string at the end of bar two (the 9th of the D major chord), then jumps over to the first string to play an A note at the 5th fret. This is the 7th of the Bb major chord and the beginning of the next chord shape.

There are two tips to take away here:

First, if we work at being able to visualise the chord shapes we're playing over, in time we'll be able to select the nearest possible note in each subsequent chord, and our melodic lines will sound much more connected. This is a long term project, but it's worth persevering with.

Secondly, when faced with a colourful chord containing alterations like the Bbmaj7#11, we don't have to wrack our brains and think, "What note is the #11?" – the root, 3rd, 5th and 7th are all safe tones we can use that will still make the sound of the chord. If you're put on the spot with an impromptu solo, you can always fall back on these safe tones, and you'll still sound like you know what you're doing!

When working through *Triste* and *Wave*, take some time to study the notes Martin chooses to move from one chord change to the next, and work out which intervals he chooses to highlight.

Get the Audio

The audio files for this book are available to download for free from **www.fundamental-changes.com.** The link is in the top right-hand corner. Click on the Guitar link then simply select this book title from the drop-down menu and follow the instructions to get the audio.

We recommend that you download the files directly to your computer, not to your tablet, and extract them there before adding them to your media library. On the download page there are instructions, and we also provide technical support via the contact form.

For over 350 free guitar lessons with videos check out:

www.fundamental-changes.com

Join our free Facebook Community of Cool Musicians

www.facebook.com/groups/fundamentalguitar

Tag us for a share on Instagram: **FundamentalChanges**

Chapter One: The Girl from Ipanema

When I think about *The Girl from Ipanema*, I'm immediately drawn into its seductive world of rhythm and melody. This tune is a masterclass in the use of intervals, particularly the major sixth, ninth, and major seventh. These intervals are the essence of what makes this song so captivating. They bring a certain sexy quality to the music. It's like a musical martini: smooth and sophisticated, with just the right amount of kick.

Playing *The Girl from Ipanema* is like telling a story. From the moment those first three notes hit – a 9th, a major 7th, and a 6th – you know exactly where you are: in the heart of Latin jazz, enveloped in a sound that's as sultry as it is elegant. The harmonies are simple yet profound, and they create the perfect musical "sandwich" where each ingredient complements the others perfectly.

What I've always admired about this piece, beyond its harmonic beauty, is its structure. It's a journey from light to shade and back again, which captures the essence of the era when Bossa Nova met North American jazz. It's this blend that makes the song the perfect introduction to the Bossa Nova.

The structure of the song is simple yet clever. It gives you a lift and takes you on a bit of a journey. There's an ascending feel in the bridge that always gets me. It's sophisticated but not complicated, which is a fine line. That's what I like about it. It's easy on the ears but gives you enough to chew on harmonically.

In my performances, I aim to capture that essence and do justice to its rich musicality while adding my own touch. It's about striking the balance between staying true to the charm of the original while bringing out my own voice within the song. It's about capturing that Bossa Nova feel – keeping it light but rhythmic – while letting the melody flow. It's a tune that lets you play around a bit with the rhythm, experiment with the intervals, and really get into the groove of the music.

And really, that's the challenge and the joy of playing music like this. We find ways to connect with the song and, by extension, with our audience. It's all about feeling it out, finding that balance between sticking to the melody and adding our own spin.

So, when you learn this solo, focus on the intervals I choose to play and the mood they create. Dive into the melody, feel the rhythm, and let it take you where it wants to go. It's more than just playing notes, it's about creating a feeling.

The Girl From Ipanema

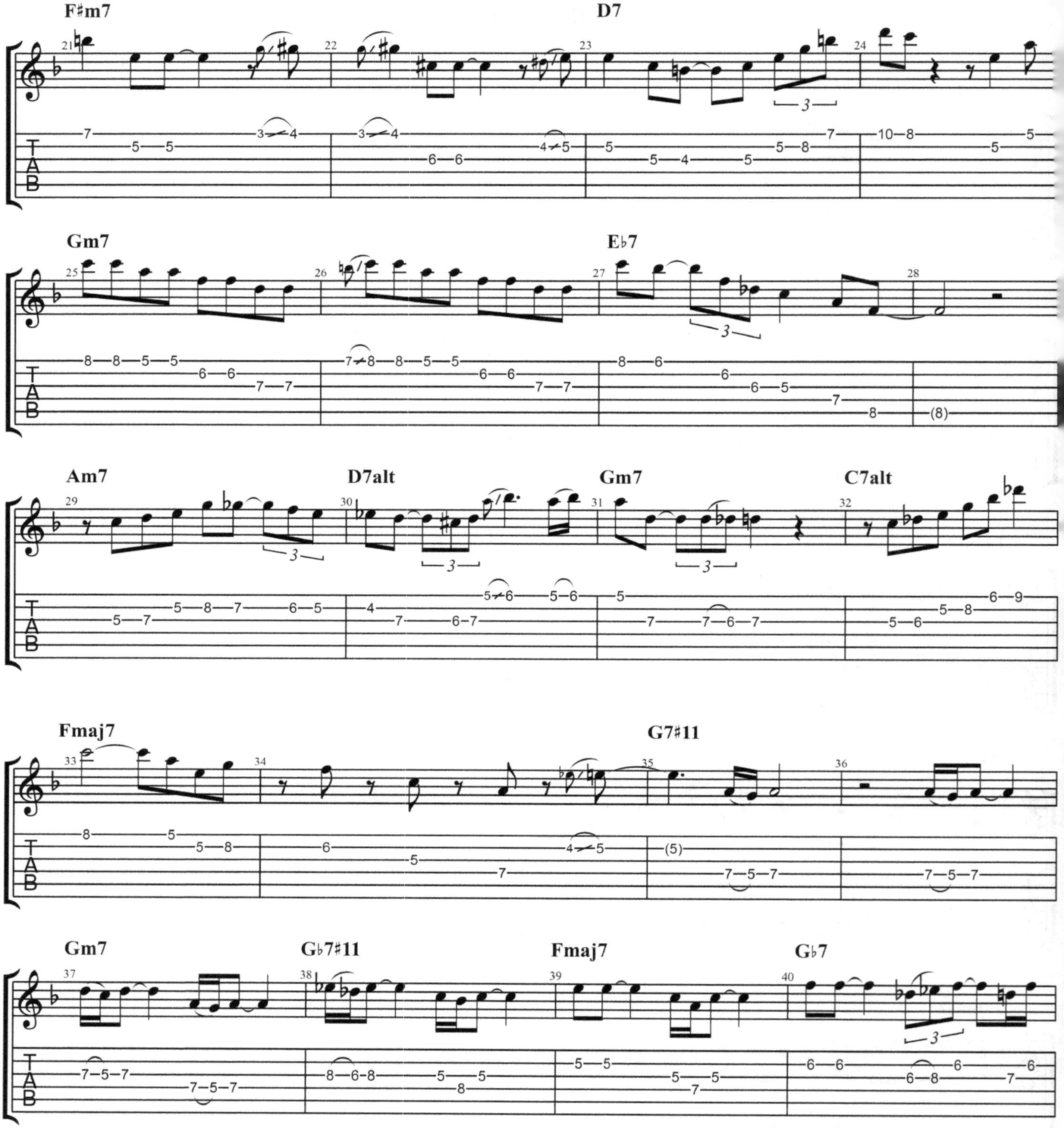
F♯m7
D7
Gm7
E♭7
Am7
D7alt
Gm7
C7alt
Fmaj7
G7♯11
Gm7
G♭7♯11
Fmaj7
G♭7

Fmaj7
G7♯11
Gm7
G♭7♯11
Fmaj7
G♭7
Fmaj7
G7♯11
Gm7
G♭7♯11
Fmaj7
F♯maj7
B7

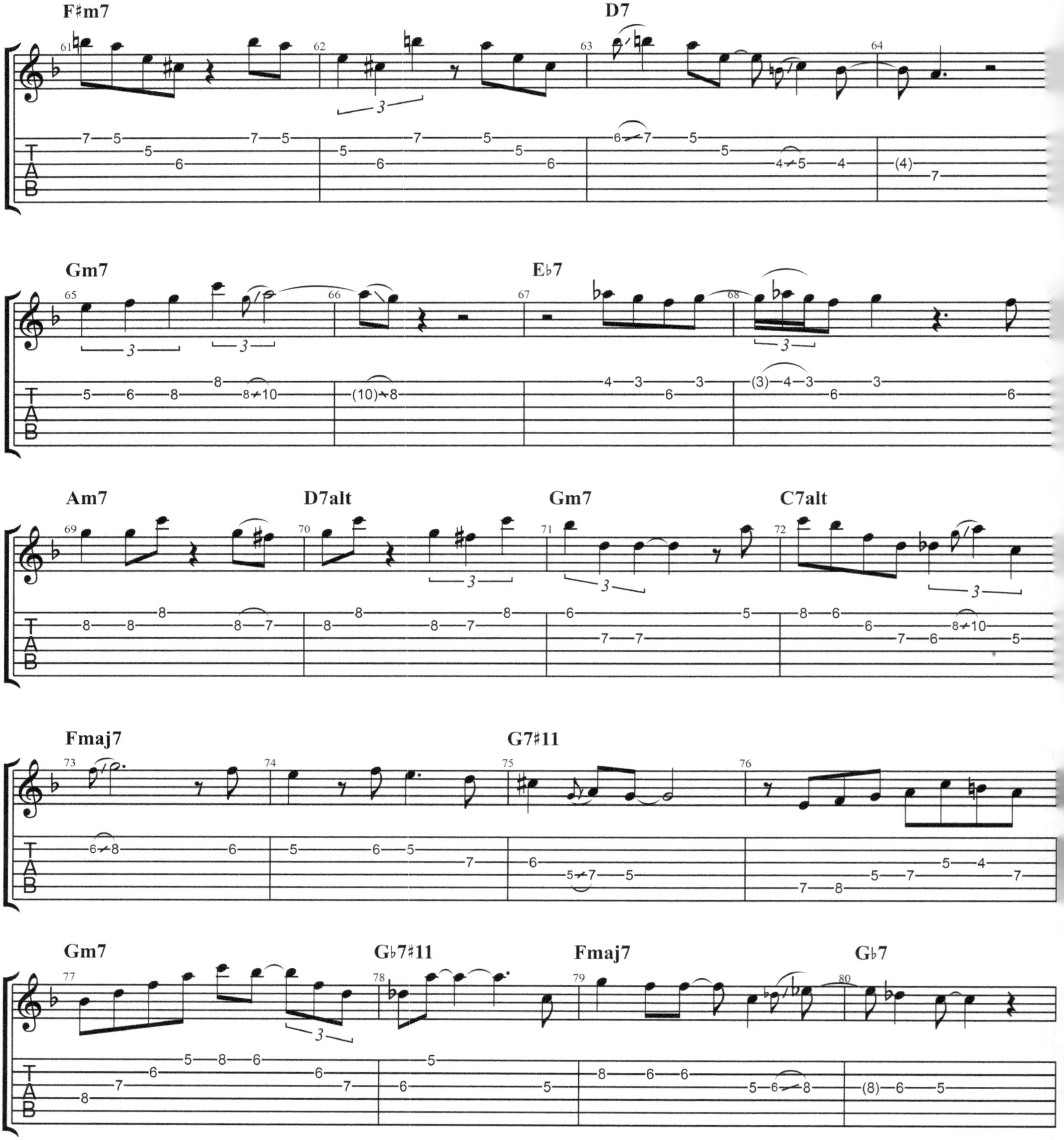
F♯m7
D7
Gm7
E♭7
Am7
D7alt
Gm7
C7alt
Fmaj7
G7♯11
Gm7
G♭7♯11
Fmaj7
G♭7

Fmaj7
G7♯11
Gm7
G♭7♯11
Fmaj7
G♭7
Fmaj7
G7♯11
Gm7
G♭7♯11
Fmaj7
F♯maj7
B7

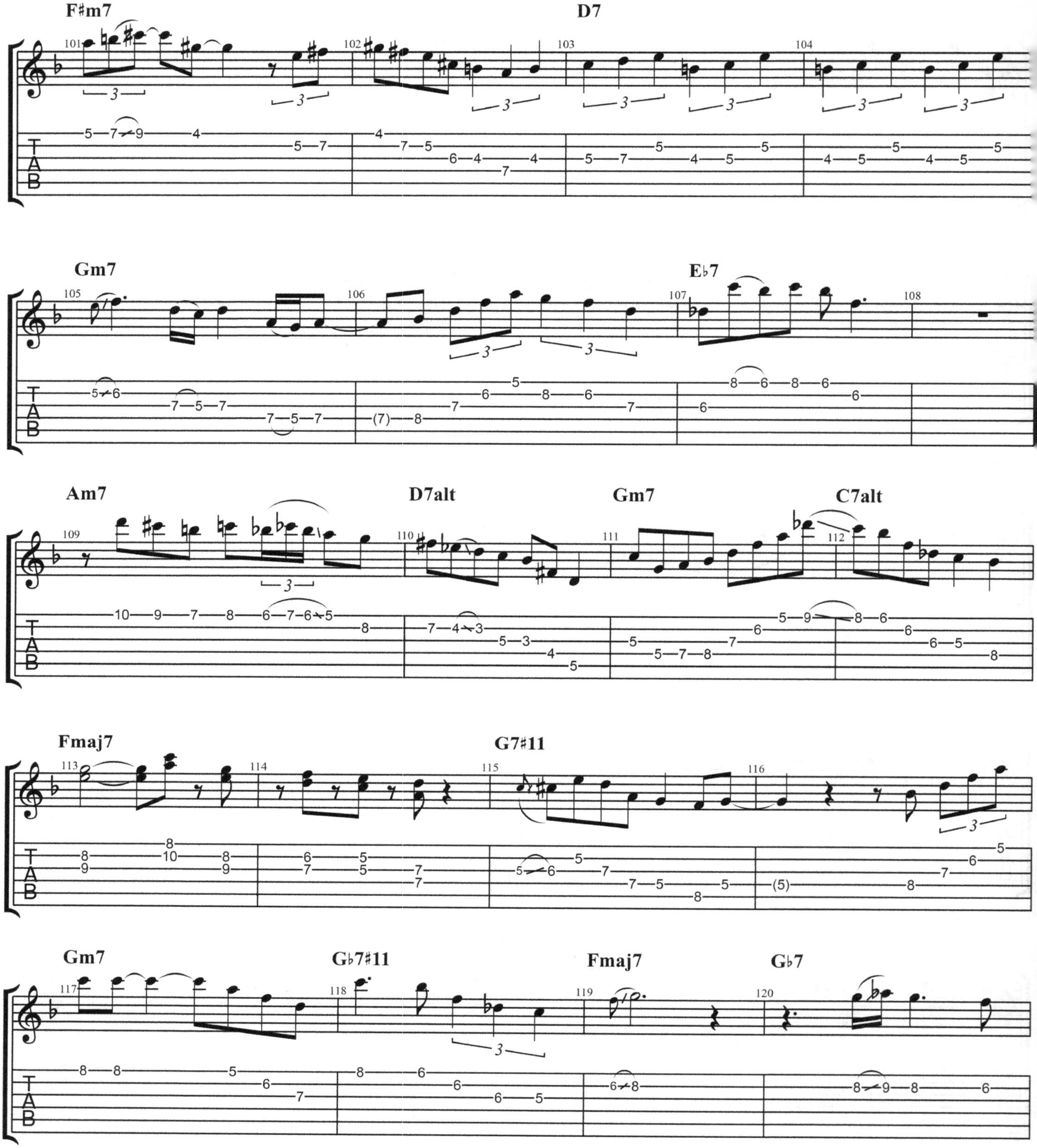
F♯m7
D7
Gm7
E♭7
Am7
D7alt
Gm7
C7alt
Fmaj7
G7♯11
Gm7
G♭7♯11
Fmaj7
G♭7

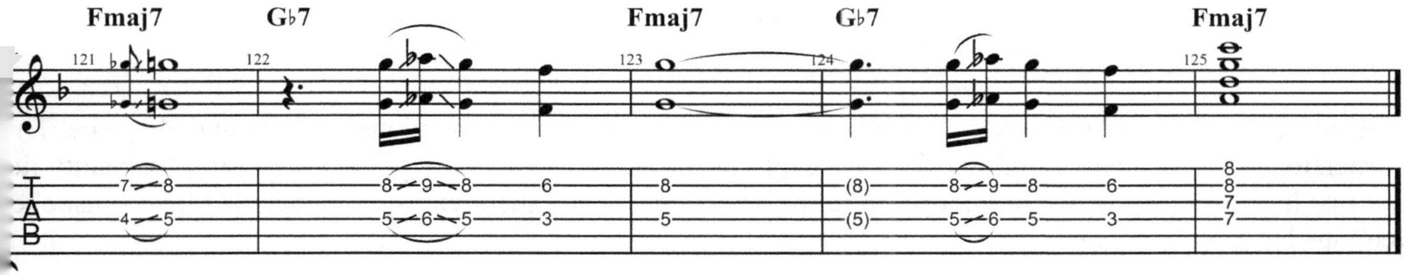
Fmaj7
G♭7
Fmaj7
G♭7
Fmaj7

Chapter Two: How Insensitive

Whenever I play *How Insensitive*, I quickly become absorbed by its profound melancholy and elegance. This cornerstone of Bossa Nova unfolds with a deceptive simplicity and a gentle yet insistent pull. Its beauty lies not just in the melody or the harmony, but in the spaces between – the breaths of silence that leave unspoken feelings hanging in the air.

Playing this tune really brings you into the essence of Bossa Nova. It has a certain flow that seems to guide you through, making it almost instinctive once you get into it. It's interesting because, despite its apparent simplicity, there are these little twists in the harmonic sequence that keep it engaging. It's this mix of straightforward rhythm combined with moments that require careful attention that I find particularly compelling.

For anyone delving into Bossa Nova, *How Insensitive* serves as a perfect entry point. It's simple enough to grasp but filled with subtleties that challenge and deepen your understanding of this genre. Harmonically, you've got to be on your toes. There have been moments, for instance, when I've mistaken a major for a minor and it's these nuances that highlight the song's depth beyond its surface simplicity.

Interestingly, the minor key doesn't make this song sound melancholy. Instead, there's a lightness, a kind of optimism woven through it. That balance is crucial. It's about capturing and conveying the inherent emotion without tipping too far into sadness, maintaining a feel that is both reflective and uplifting.

The chord sequence is straightforward, yet laden with subtle shifts that demand attention and care as each transition feels like a step deeper into the story. The song's structure creates a narrative arc that is both universally recognisable and intensely personal. To play *How Insensitive* is to navigate the intricacies of human emotion as they are translated into music.

This song teaches us the value of restraint; of the power held in a single note that's played with true feeling. It teaches the importance of dynamics – of how to use silence as effectively as sound – and of holding back and waiting for the right moment to release a note, allowing its heartache and beauty to shine.

In essence, tackling *How Insensitive* is not just about technical play, it's about immersing yourself in the mood of the piece, exploring its depth, and bringing that to the listeners. It's a tune that despite, or perhaps because of, its complexities, remains a joy to play, offering a window into the intricate dance of Bossa Nova's rhythmic and harmonic interplay.

Approaching this piece, I encourage you to feel the rhythm and let the harmonies guide you, but above all, allow the emotion of the song to flow through your playing. My hope is that you'll find your own path through its beauty and sadness, and that you'll discover something new about yourself.

How Insensitive

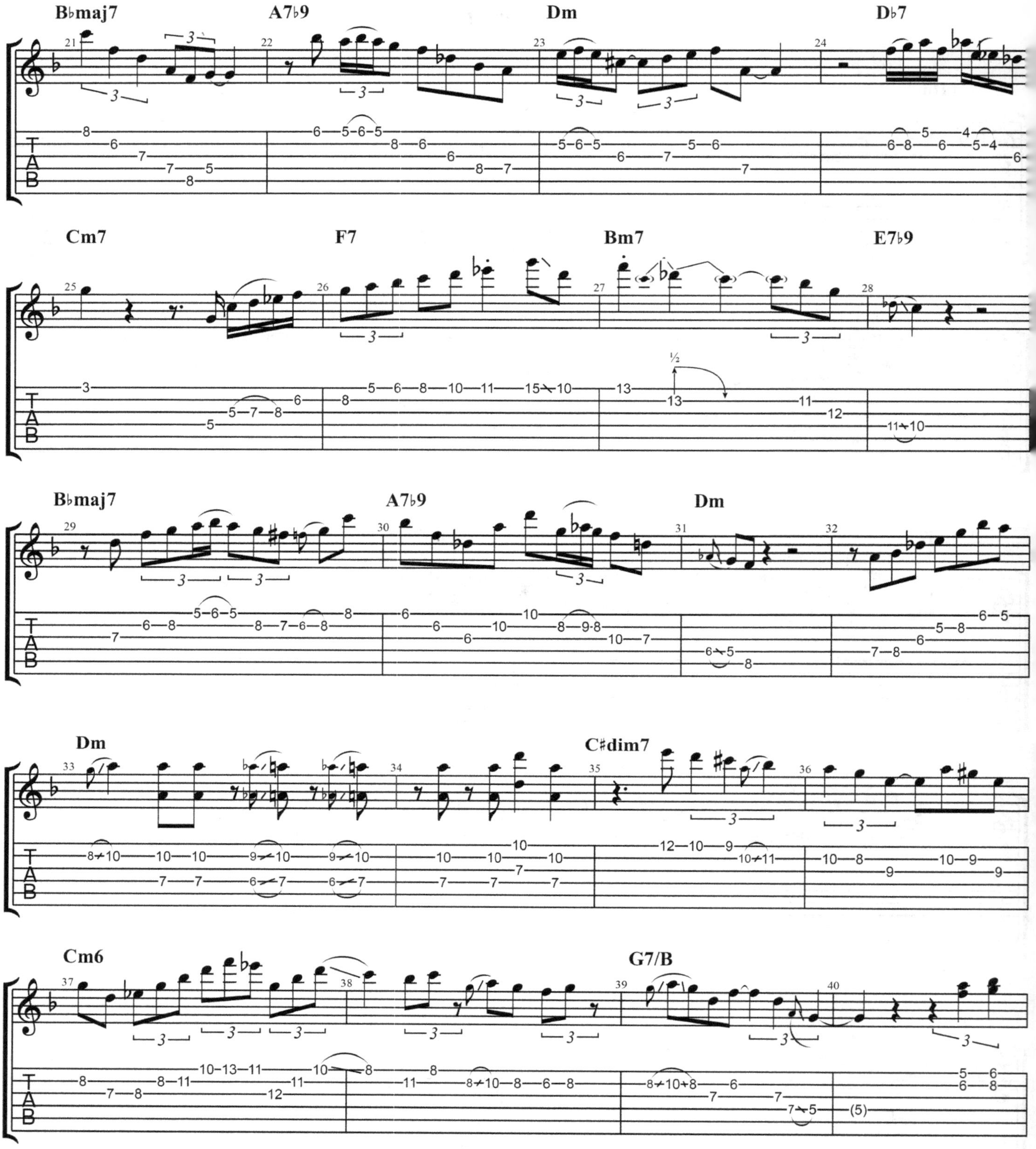
B♭maj7
A7♭9
Dm
D♭7
Cm7
F7
Bm7
E7♭9
B♭maj7
A7♭9
Dm
Dm
C♯dim7
Cm6
G7/B

B♭maj7
E♭maj7♯11
E7
A7♭9
Dm
D♭7
Cm6
Bdim7
B♭maj7
A7♭9
Dm
D♭7
Cm7
F7
Bm7
E7♭9

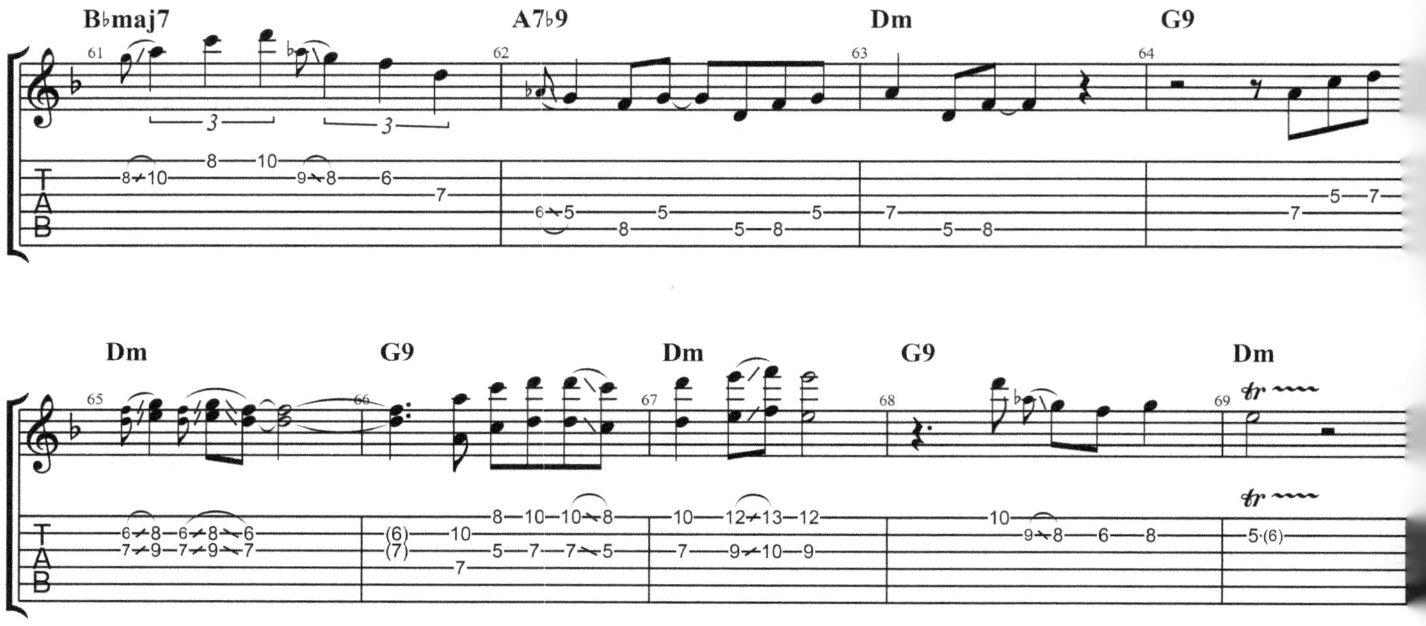
B♭maj7
A7♭9
Dm
G9
Dm
G9
Dm
G9
Dm

Chapter Three: Keep the Home Fires Burning

Keep the Home Fires Burning has a special place in my set, particularly because of its historical context and the unique challenge it posed for adaptation to Latin guitar.

The original song, from the First World War era, carries a message of hope and resilience that I find deeply moving and still relevant today. Adapting it into a Latin guitar context was not just about changing its rhythm or adding a different flavour, it was about respecting its essence while exploring new musical landscapes.

When adapting this piece, my focus was on maintaining the integrity of its melody and the emotional weight it carries. The chord structure is simple, which gave me some flexibility in reimagining it for Latin guitar. But that also meant that every note, every chord change, had to be carefully considered to ensure the song's original sentiment wasn't lost in translation.

This process involved experimenting with various Latin rhythms and chord voicings that could complement the original melody without overpowering it. The challenge was to find a balance that would preserve the song's narrative, while introducing a new dimension that could offer a fresh perspective. The goal was to create a version that felt both familiar and new. Playing this piece requires a delicate touch, as you blend the melodic phrasing and Latin dynamics with the song's poignant melody.

In bringing *Keep the Home Fires Burning* into my repertoire, I aimed to offer audiences a unique listening experience that honoured the past while embracing the richness of Latin music. It's a testament to the enduring power of music to convey emotions and stories across generations, and I'm proud to share this adaptation with you, so that you can explore its depth and beauty through a new lens.

Keep the Home Fires Burning

C#m7
G#7
Amaj7
A#m7♭5
D#7
G#m7
C#m7
G7
F#7
B7sus
Emaj7
B7sus
Emaj7
D#m7♭5
G#7alt
C#m7
G#7
TAB

Amaj7
A♯m7♭5
D♯7
G♯m7
C♯m7
G7
F♯7
F♯m7
B7sus
Emaj7
D♯m7♭5
G♯7alt
C♯m7
G7
Amaj7
A♯m7♭5
D♯7
G♯m7
C♯m7
G7

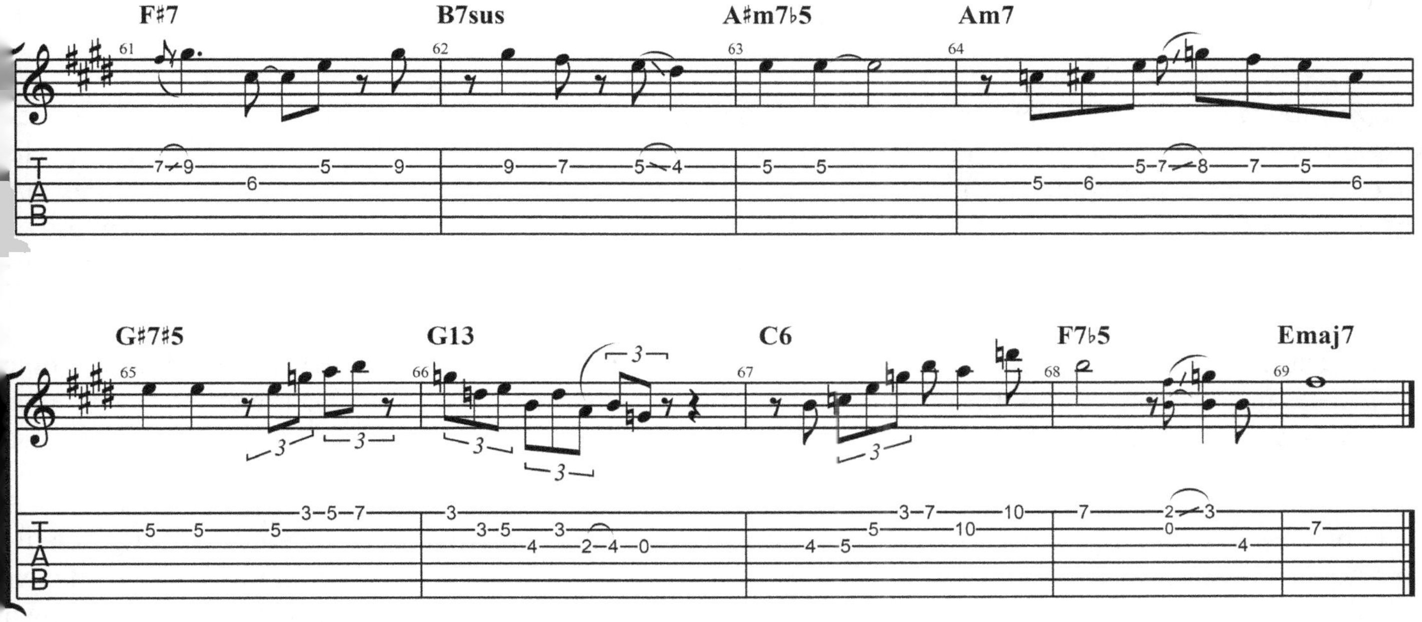
F♯7
B7sus
A♯m7♭5
Am7
G♯7♯5
G13
C6
F7♭5
Emaj7

Chapter Four: Night and Day

Night and Day is a tune I've long incorporated into my repertoire. It's one of those jazz standards that has been played in many different styles and at different speeds, but fits very well into the Bossa Nova tradition. The decision to play it this way wasn't arbitrary. The song itself, while not originally a Bossa, has qualities that naturally lend themselves to the genre. This realization came to me over the years, and was somewhat reinforced when Diana Krall released her Bossa Nova version of the tune on her *Quiet Nights* ablum, highlighting its compatibility with the style.

In my experience, many songs, even those not originally intended as Bossa Novas, have underlying harmonic sequences that surprisingly suit the rhythm and feel of Latin music, and *Night and Day* is a prime example. Its chord progression, particularly the way the bridge lifts with a minor third, lends itself beautifully to a Bossa Nova interpretation, and gives that uplifting yet melancholic feel characteristic of the genre.

The process of adapting any jazz standard isn't just about changing its rhythm, but about exploring how its harmonic structure can be accentuated by the Bossa Nova style. This conversion from one style to another highlights how great music can transcend genres, and how new flavours can be brought out of well-known tunes. It's a testament to this song's versatility and the richness of Bossa Nova as a musical form.

The interplay between jazz and other musical cultures has always fascinated me, and *Night and Day* serves as the perfect example of this musical exchange. Its adaptation into Bossa Nova reflects the broader dialogue between American jazz and Brazilian music – a relationship that has enriched both genres. This song, with its complex harmonies and engaging melody, is the beautiful result of such a cultural exchange.

This approach is a reflection of my belief in the power of music to bridge worlds, to innovate within tradition, and to continually find fresh ways to fuse genres.

Night and Day

Bmaj7
B♭7
E♭maj7
Am7♭5
A♭m7
Gm7
F♯m7
Fm7
B♭7
E♭maj7
G♭maj7
E♭maj7
G♭maj7
E♭maj7

Am7♭5
A♭m7
Gm7
F♯m7
Fm7
B♭7
E♭maj7
Bmaj7
B♭7
E♭maj7
Bmaj7
B♭7
E♭maj7
Am7♭5
A♭m7
Gm7
F♯m7

Fm7
B♭7
E♭maj7
Bmaj7
B♭7
E♭maj7
Bmaj7
B♭7
E♭maj7
Am7♭5
A♭m7
Gm7
F♯m7
Fm7
B♭7
E♭maj7

G♭maj7
E♭maj7
G♭maj7
E♭maj7
Am7♭5
A♭m7
Gm7
F♯m7
Fm7
B♭7
E♭maj7
D♭7
E♭maj7

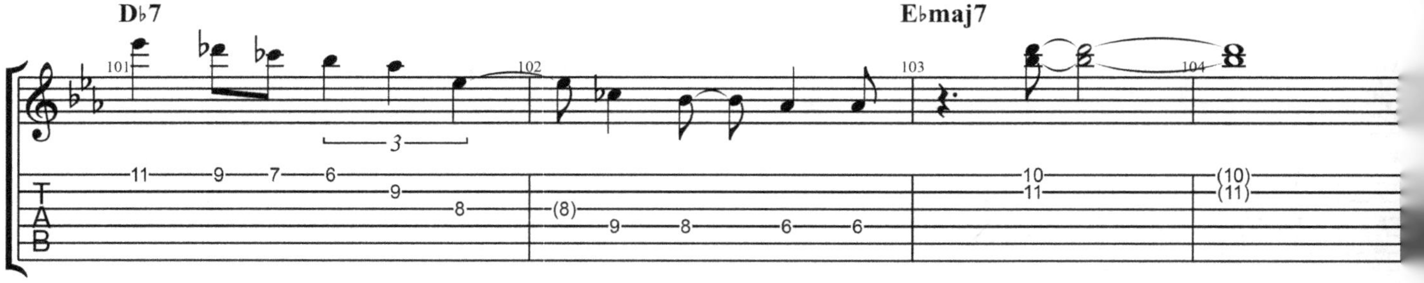
D♭7
E♭maj7

Chapter Five: The Shadow of Your Smile

The Shadow of Your Smile shares a mood and sentiment similar to *How Insensitive*, which is something I've always appreciated. It's fascinating how the song, once you start to play it, carries itself with a kind of inner momentum. It's not just the melody – the whole harmonic sequence just flows beautifully, making it a joy to play. Even though this is another jazz standard that wasn't originally a Bossa Nova, it has adapted so well to the Latin style over the years that it's frequently played this way and has found its place in the repertoire.

The interesting thing is how well the song's inherent mood translates into this new context. Despite its minor key, which typically creates a sad mood, the Latin treatment gives it a lighter, more uplifting feel. This balance between the song's original melancholy and its Bossa Nova adaptation highlights the depth and complexity that can be explored within a seemingly simple tune.

My approach involves more than just navigating through its chord progressions, it's about capturing and conveying the song's emotional landscape. This involves a careful consideration of melody, harmony, and rhythm to ensure that the essence of the original piece shines through, even as it's presented in a different musical style.

It's this process of exploration and interpretation that I find particularly rewarding, offering a new perspective on a well-loved standard. It's another reminder of music's power to transcend genres and eras, connecting with listeners by virtue of its universal themes and melodies. It highlights the song's enduring appeal and the ongoing conversation between musical traditions.

The Shadow of Your Smile

Am7
D7
Bm7♭5
E7♭9
Am7
Cm7
Bm7
E7alt
A7
D7sus
G6
B7♭9
F♯m7
B7♭9
Em7
A7
Am7
D7
Gmaj7
Cmaj7

F♯m7♭5
B7♭9
Em7
Em/D
C♯m7♭5
F♯7♭9
F♯m7♭5
B7alt
F♯m7
B7♭9
Em7
A7
Am7
D7
Bm7♭5
E7♭9
Am7
Cm7
Bm7
E7alt
TAB

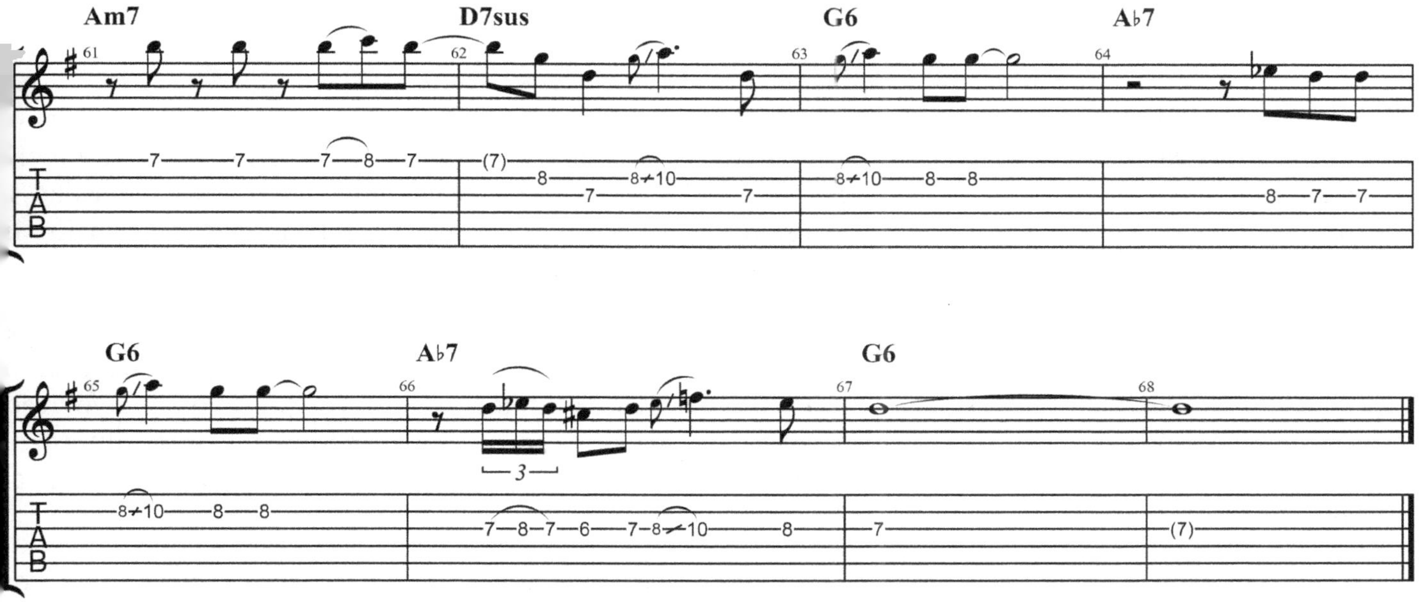
Am7
D7sus
G6
A♭7
G6
A♭7
G6

Chapter Six: Triste

The word *Triste*, meaning "sad" in Italian, sets the stage for this piece. It's fascinating how a song written in a minor key can capture a melancholy mood, yet when approached with a Latin treatment takes on a more reflective mood, rather than sinking into despair. The Latin rhythms inject some sunlight into the sadness, showcasing how the same melody can evoke different emotions in different musical contexts. This duality is what drew me to explore the song further and integrate it into my performances.

Triste is an interesting piece from a guitarist's perspective, and improvising on it is an immersive process due to its harmonic richness. The song is laden with ii-V-I cadences – the staple chord progression of hundreds of jazz standards, which opens up so many possibilities for melodic exploration. As you play, you find yourself weaving through the harmony, playing with the tension and release that these progressions naturally offer. Developing a vocabulary of licks to play over these changes is rewarding, as varying them offers great expressive freedom.

This piece can be played at different tempos depending on the feel you wish to create. My approach leans towards a slightly faster rendition, which I find brings out a fresher character in the music.

It's important to really feel the tempo of a piece before diving in; to let it sit in your body. Sometimes, imagining just one phrase of the song can guide you to its ideal tempo and set the pace for the entire performance.

For me, *Triste* embodies the beauty of music's ability to convey complex emotions through simple changes in rhythm and harmony. It showcases the guitar's expressive capacity to tell a story without words. As I play, I aim to take listeners on a journey that acknowledges the sadness of the tune but also offers a sense of hope through its Latin interpretation.

Triste

Dmaj7
Am7
D7
Gmaj7
C7
F♯m7
B7
E7
Em7
A7
Dm7
G7
Dm7
G7
Dm7
G7
Dm7
G7
Dmaj7
B♭maj7
Dmaj7

F♯m7
B7
Em7
C♯m7
F♯7
Bm7
C♯7
F♯maj7
G♯m7
C♯7
F♯maj7
B7
Em7
A7
Dmaj7
Dm7
G7
Dmaj7
Am7
D7
Gmaj7
C7

F♯m7 B7 E7 Em7 A7
Dm7 G7 Dm7 G7 Dm7 G7 Dm7 G7
Dm7 G7 Dm7 G7 Dm7 G7 Dm7 G7
Dmaj7

Chapter Seven: Wave

Wave is right up there with *The Girl from Ipanema* and *How Insensitive* as one of those songs everyone plays when they're exploring Bossa Nova.

It has its challenges when you're called to improvise over it, but that's what makes it interesting. When soloing on *Wave*, a lot of it comes down understanding the harmonic progression of the song, and especially that Bbdim7 chord in bar two! This chord is crucial because it sets a unique mood, and you need to know how to navigate it to make your improvisation flow.

It's useful to know that Bbdim7 can be seen as a *substitution* for an A7 chord. In fact, if you put all of the notes of Bbdim7 over an A bass note, you create an A7b9 sound. It's therefore useful to think of the chord sequence as DMaj9 – A7b9 – Am7 – D7, which makes it a little easier to digest and improvise over.

Diminished chords like this have a rich history in jazz, though they've become less common over time. In *Wave*, the diminished chord provides a distinctive twist early in the song, which is something you don't always see. When improvising, we can be mindful of this and use it to our advantage.

Diminished chords can be tricky to navigate because there's always the temptation to just play the arpeggio up and down. Instead, I tend to stick close to the chord when improvising. I don't add chromatic passing notes, as they can be too dissonant around a diminished chord. It's about sticking close to the structure of the chord while also finding your own path through it.

The piece is also full of common elements like ii–Vs, but there are some unexpected key changes, so you have to be on your toes.

When I solo on *Wave*, I aim to bring my own voice to the music within the framework it provides. It's a challenge, but one that's rewarding and deeply engaging.

Wave

E7
A7
Dm9
G13
Gm7
C9
Fmaj7
Fm7
B♭7
E♭maj7
A7alt
Dmaj7
B♭dim7
Am7
D9
Gmaj7
Gm6
F♯7
B7

E9 A7 Dm9 G13 Dm9 G13
Dmaj7 B♭dim7 Am7 D9
Gmaj7 Gm6 F♯7 B7
E9 A7 Dm9 G13 Dm9 G13
Dmaj7 B♭dim7 Am7 D9

Gmaj7
Gm6
F♯7
B7
E9
A7
Dm9
G13
Dm9
G13
Gm7
C9
Fmaj7
Fm7
B♭7
E♭maj7
A7alt
Dmaj7
B♭dim7
Am7
D9

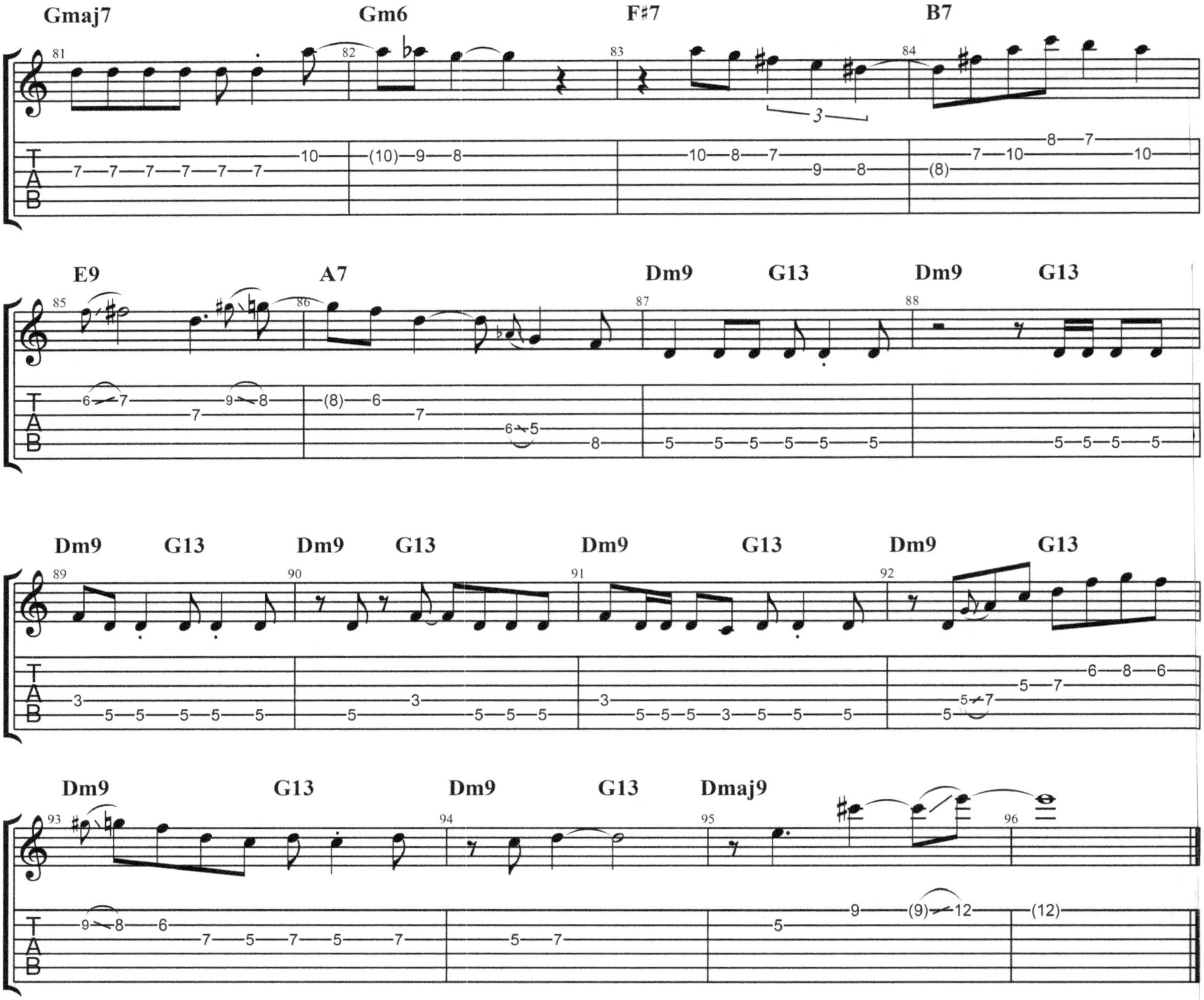

Conclusion

As we wrap up this book, I want to share some thoughts on how you can take what you've learned and start creating your own solos. What I've aimed to show through these tunes is not just a series of chord sequences and melodies, but a way to see beyond them. To see the potential for your own musical expression within these frameworks.

Many musicians struggle with a kind of mental block when it comes to crafting their own music. They feel like they need to find something completely out of the ordinary to make their mark. But the reality is, the foundation for your own tunes, your own solos, is closer than you think. It's woven into the chords and melodies you're already familiar with. Every great composer has started from somewhere, often by exploring the familiar and then branching out.

So, how do you start?

It begins with not overthinking it. You don't have to leap straight to the musical equivalent of Mount Everest. Start simple. Play around with the melodies, vary them, see where they lead you. If you get stuck, step back from trying to be a "guitar player" for a moment. Instead, be a musician. Sing a bit. Hum. Find a phrase that catches your ear and build from there.

This process isn't just about theory or technique, it's deeply musical. It's about finding a melody that speaks to you, then developing it, and organizing it into a structure that resonates. And remember, don't let the guitar dictate where you go – you're in control. You play the guitar; don't let the guitar play you!

Think of completing this book as your basecamp. You've learned the solos, you've seen how they're constructed, now it's time to start climbing. Use what you've learned as a springboard. Find your melody, your harmony, maybe even your countermelody, and see where they take you.

If there's one thing I hope you take away from this book, it's the confidence to start experimenting with your own music. Don't get bogged down thinking you need to reinvent the wheel. Music, at its core, is about expression and connection, not just innovation for its own sake.

So, where do you go from here?

Start with the melodies and chord progressions you've learned. Play around with them, see what new directions they might take you. And don't be afraid to just sing! Sometimes, stepping away from the guitar and using your voice can spark new ideas and help you break free from falling into the same familiar patterns.

Finally, remember, it's all music, and music is a vast, unexplored territory waiting for your footprint. So, take a deep breath, and let's see where your music takes you!

Martin

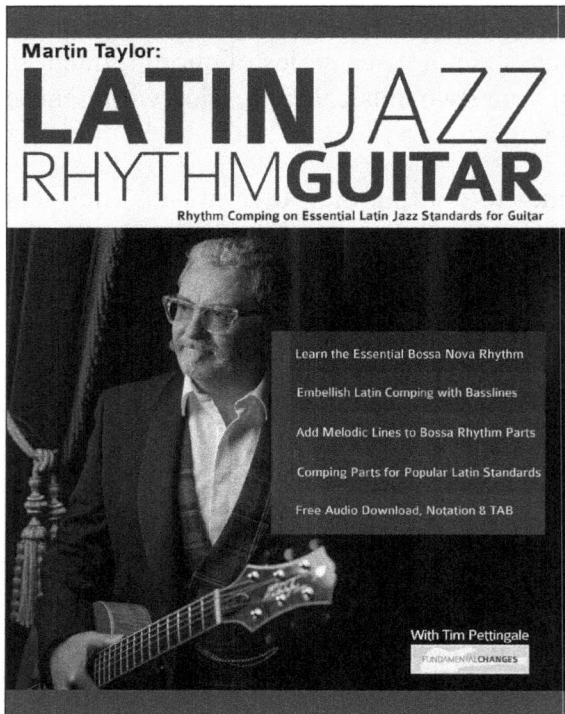

Discover Latin Jazz Rhythm Guitar with Martin Taylor

Ready to learn the art of Latin Jazz guitar?

In Martin Taylor's Latin Jazz Rhythm Guitar, iconic guitar virtuoso Dr Martin Taylor shows you how to quickly master the basic bossa groove, then transform it into endless musical comping patterns.

Part One – Boss Nova Guitar from the Ground Up

For those new to Latin Jazz, have no fear – this book begins with an easy-to-follow, practical guide to nailing the bossa nova groove and breaking it down beat by beat.

Next, using the bossa groove as your foundation, you'll quickly learn to embellish the basic rhythm to add endless variations and nuances.

- Use compact chord grips to free up fingers to play embellishments and melody
- Add subtle chord accent variations to break free from boring patterns
- Get grooving by creating bassline and adding push / pull rhythms
- Easily add melodies on the top two strings
- Play musical inner lines to add harmonic movement

With dozens of practical examples, you'll learn Martin's favourite musical decorations to common chord grips and quickly use them in your own playing.

Part Two – A Masterclass in Chord Embellishment

In Part Two you'll learn Martin's stunning chord embellishments and how to apply them to the greatest Latin Jazz tunes ever written.

You'll learn how Martin plays these Antônio Carlos Jobim classics:

- The Girl from Ipanema
- Wave
- Corcovado (Quiet Nights)
- Triste
- How Insensitive

Plus, two classic standards often played in the Latin Jazz style:

- The Shadow of Your Smile
- Night and Day

You'll also discover Martin's original arrangement of the classic Keep the Home Fires Burning, and learn how any tune with a strong melody can be given the bossa nova guitar treatment.

In Martin Taylor's Latin Jazz Rhythm Guitar, you'll learn hundreds of fresh ideas you can use in your own rhythm playing immediately.

Bonus 1: Handy chord substitution ideas to take your tunes to the next level and make them easier to play!

Bonus 2: Martin's unique tweaks to classic tunes that you won't find in the Real Book

Bonus 3: Martin's exclusive advice on how to practice any tune you want, bossa style

With clear TAB and notation, along with dozens of audio tracks you can download for free, you won't find a deeper guide to Latin Jazz guitar, from a true master of the craft.

Martin Taylor's Latin Jazz Rhythm Guitar is your chance to sit down with a master and learn beautiful chord phrases you'll be playing for years to come!